What people are saying...

"*This book is chockfull of practical and easy-to-implement tips, tools, and techniques for your trade show success. From simple table-top to custom exhibits, the principles Richard shares can help you get a significant return on your trade show investment.*"

Susan Friedmann, CSP, international bestselling author of *Riches in Niches: How to Make it BIG in a small Market.*

"*Richard Avdoian takes the mystery out of succeeding at a trade show. This book provides a powerful, practical and proven blueprint to help companies successfully convert prospects into new customers at their next trade show or Expo.*"

Ron Ameln, CEO, *St. Louis Small Business Monthly*

"*If you are responsible for building ROI into the next trade show you exhibit at, you must not only read this book, but also use the guides and advice. This field-tested guidebook shows exactly how to prepare, set up and succeed at your next trade show.*"

Joe Clote, Owner, Trade Show Producer and Publisher of *Meet Missouri*, *Meet Kansas*, and *Meet Med*© magazines.

"*Richard Avdoian has written an absolute must-read guidebook for anyone considering trade shows. This guidebook covers how to select and train the idea trade show team and how to prepare and succeed at your next Expo or trade show.*"

Andy Blanton V.P. of Sales, Xtreme Exhibits | Nimlok St Louis

Successfully Working Trade Shows

Practical Tips to Attract New Clients, Strengthen Your Brand, and Make More Sales

Richard Avdoian, CSP™

Falls Street Press

Successfully Working Trade Shows
Practical Tips to Attract New Clients, Strengthen Your Brand, and Make More Sales
Richard Avdoian
Falls Street Press

Published by Falls Street Press
Copyright ©2022 Richard Avdoian
All rights reserved.

Cover and Interior design: Davis Creative Publishing Partners, CreativePublishingPartners.com

ISBN: 979-8-9855158-1-7

1. BUS020000   BUSINESS & ECONOMICS / Development / Business Development
   2. BUS002000   BUSINESS & ECONOMICS / Advertising & Promotion   3. REF032000
   REFERENCE / Event Planning

LCCN 2022909977

2022

Special Thanks

Ron Ameln, CEO, *St. Louis Small Business Monthly*

Andy Blanton, V.P. of Sales, Xtreme Exhibits

Steven Iversen, CSP™, CEO & President, Aurora Pointe

Patrick Donadio, CSP™, MCC

for their helpful contributions and suggestions.

Jack Davis, Davis Creative Publishing Partners
for his patience, expertise, and assistance.

Table of Contents

Foreword

Put Your Company In Front Of Hundreds of Prospects

GET LEADS - BUILD SALES - INCREASE REVENUE

Why Should You Exhibit At The Expo?

Do you have a product and/or service you want to share with thousands of businesses?

With an ***average 2,000+*** attendees looking for new vendor solutions at each event, your Company will get massive brand exposure and the opportunity to make on-the-spot sales.

Exhibiting at an Expo is more than just advertising – it is active marketing directly to Company Decision-Makers who are specifically shopping for products & services just like yours. There is no better place that you can connect with thousands of motivated buyers and cultivate new business opportunities in one day.

Reasons to Exhibit:

- Meet hundreds of business owners who attend specifically to find ways to run better businesses. Where else can you meet so many decision makers in one day?
- Network with hundreds of potential new customers.
- Demonstrate your product or service in a live setting.
- Shorten your sales cycle…meet your next customers face to face
- Conduct real business on the show floor
- Gain direct market feedback as you discuss your products/ services directly with prospects

- Build your brand as new customers discover you.
- Launch new products or services.
- Target your geographic market and increase sales immediately

Ron Ameln, CEO
St. Louis Small Business Monthly

Introduction
Trade Shows Are Not A Waste Of Time

Tradeshows and expos provide many opportunities to meet your next business partner or customer, visit vendors who provide services and products to businesses, attend business seminars and exchange business cards with other attendees.

For years, when the economy was strong, businesses and professionals could get away with doing what they have always done to attract business and prosper. As they say, those were the good old days. Today customers are reaching new companies and service providers less by word of mouth and more through the internet, tradeshows and social media. Companies need to shift their focus and marketing from hunting for new customers to being hunted. Tradeshows are a great venue to showcase your expertise and expose your company to business owners and professionals hunting for services and products.

I have heard many companies and professionals complain about the low ROI from participating in tradeshows given the investment in time and money. It really doesn't have to be the case if properly prepared. For tradeshows to be cost-effective and to increase your ROI consider these tips.

Start promoting the day you commit to participating in the show. Create a few variations of email blasts promoting your participation in the expo starting with a save-the-date, followed by a few others sent two to three weeks apart to your prospects, clients, colleagues and family and friends. Each blast should appear as a special invitation: "I would like to personally invite you…"; "Please join me…."; "I am excited to announce…".

Inquire about possible speaking opportunities. It never hurts to inquire as many tradeshows offer free seminars presented by exhibitors. These opportunities offer one more opportunity to really position your business as a leader and expert in your industry. Typically, seminars range from 45 to 60 minutes. The focus of the seminar should not be about your business but rather about sharing your expertise related to your industry and target niches.

Make sure your booth design is appealing. The visual appearance of your booth is the porthole to attracting key prospects. Take the necessary time and invest the appropriate funds to design a booth that best represents your company, service and products.

Be selective when assigning employees to represent your business. Nothing will guarantee a bad experience and terrible ROI like sending members of your company who are not properly trained to effectively work a expo. Worst yet is sending employees who are not confident or knowledgeable of your services and products.

Invest the time and funds. If you are a newbie to tradeshows consider consulting with tradeshow and marketing experts to create a booth and plan in order to get the best ROI.

Chapter 1:
Do Your EXPO Homework

Expos and trade shows provide business owners, corporations and associations one of the best venues to spread and instill brand recognition, launch a new business, introduce a new product or services, develop professional relationships and gather positive leads from your target audience(s). The primary objective is not only to gain attention but to create desire, establish a relationship and get pertinent information in their hands and hopefully take action.

Trade shows can be expensive, considering travel expenses, hotel accommodations, booth cost, meals, registration fees, and employee salaries. To get the best ROI for your business, do your homework before you commit to an EXPO or trade show by reviewing this checklist:

Determine:

- What portion of your company's budget will you allocate and why?
- Your company's yearly EXPO/trade show goals, then review and revise yearly.
- Who are your best potential customers and which shows typically target these individuals?

Be selective:

- Will this show attract your target customers?
- What portion of the budget will be used for this specific show and is it worth it?
- Will it draw an audience sizeable enough to justify the investment (salaries, time, supplies etc) in exhibiting?
- Will your key competitors be exhibiting?

- Will it offer additional opportunities that will raise your visibility i.e., sponsorships, speaking venues, demonstrations?
- Invest the time to research the EXPO/trade show's history, ask questions, and develop a plan of action:

  1. Booth cost

     - Additional expenses (electricity, floor covering, internet connections etc.)
     - Primary targeted audiences
     - Typical attendance, number of vendors, etc.
     - EXPO/Trade Show Hours
     - Set-up and break-down time
     - Is there specific time for decision makers?
     - Amount of direct contact time with attendees.

  2. Have a specific agenda and plan of action

     - Will participating generate a return on my investment?
     - Target 1-3 specific measurable goals?
     - Selling
     - Positioning your brand
     - Assess this new market/event

  3. Have a creative, attractive and interactive display

     - Invest in a professionally designed and constructed booth
     - Invest the money to incorporate the trade show theme into your display
     - Routinely update photos & content
     - Replace or repair damaged or worn out portions of the display

4. Freebies, products, snacks?

- Decide whether to give out freebies, products, snacks or nothing at all
- Determine what promotional materials is suitable for the attendees

5. Select team members who are:

- Prepared to represent the company
- Knowledgeable of products and services
- Able to identify ideal prospects
- Extroverts – effective in attracting prospects

6. Create a top-notch, trained trade show team

- Invest in a professional training program for the team

7. Have a follow-up plan of action

- How will leads be gathered
- Who will make follow-up contacts
- By what means will leads be contacted
- Create time-line

Taking the time to research, plan and create an enticing interactive booth staffed by trained employees will likely lead to a great ROI.

Notes

Chapter 2:
Take Time to Think before Reacting

Trade shows can be expensive, considering travel expenses, hotel accommodations, booth cost, meals, registration fees, and employee salaries. It is estimated that a typical trade show can cost around $10,000 once all expenses are factored in. Consideration should also be made regarding time spent preparing and follow-up after the event and the loss of possible sales while at the event particularly at non-selling shows.

Additional expenses can include:

- Shipping (exhibit and supplies - In & out)
- Drayage (material handling – In & out)
- Electric (floor work – In & out)
- Installation & Dismantle
- Lead retrieval fee
- Floral rental
- Furniture rental
- Carpet rental
- Patting rental
- Internet service fee
- Cable TV rental fee

So, it is wise and good business to take the necessary time to *do your homework* before you commit to a trade show.

Determine:

- What portion of your company's budget will you allocate to trade shows and why?
- Company's yearly Trade Show goals, review and revise yearly.
- Who are your best potential customers, and which shows typically target these individuals?

Be selective:

Will this show attract your target customers?

What portion of the budget will be used for this specific show and is it worth it?

Will the show draw an audience sizeable enough to justify the investment (salaries, time, supplies etc) in exhibiting?

Will your key competitors be exhibiting?

Does the trade show offer additional opportunities that will raise your visibility i.e., sponsorships, speaking venues, demonstrations?

Chapter 3:
Before You Embark on the
Trade Show Journey Consider

- Think first then plan. Plan wel in advance, rather than react under pressure and a quick turnaround deadline. Taking the time will likely save time, money and minimize any hardships.
- Establish specific objectives. Have specific objectives for each trade show as they may vary in types of attendees and be certain the employees staffing the booth clearly understand the objectives well in advance to allow time to prepare.
- Getting your key ideal prospects to attend the trade show and specifically your booth takes three basic steps promote prior to, during, and following the trade show.
- Design an attractive, dynamic booth. All you have is approximately 7 seconds to attract attention and spark interest. The entire display must reflect positively on the company's values, personality, professionalism, and expertise.
- Team dynamics are trained teams. Attendees first experience and impression with your company is the interaction with your trade show team. So, invest in training a unified prepared team to make positive first impressions.
- Be unconventional — be creative, attendees want to be entertained as well as informed. The goal is to successfully merge both. Be playful on purpose.
- What is your key strategy? Trade show attendees base their opinion of businesses on the quality of the employees staffing the booth. The key is to invest in training those staffing the booth with a basic script that allows for

personalization that engages and prompts prospects curiosity and additional questions.

- Have a follow-up plan to established with deadlines. Now the real work begins implementing your plan. Prior to the trade show develop a few email templates and determine what you plan to fax or mail the most promising prospects that enhances interest and solicits an appointment.

Trade shows provide business owners, associations, and corporations one of the best venues to launch and spread brand recognition, develop professional relationships, and gather positive leads from their target audience(s). The primary objective is not to simply get their attention but to create desire, make a connection laying the foundation to establish a relationship and get pertinent information in their hands to review later and hopefully consider taking serious action.

Chapter 4:
Keep In Mind to be Successful –
Be Creative, Focused and Engaged

Trade Shows aren't cheap

- Airfare, employee pay, booth design and registration
- Loss of sales – while attending the event
- Time spent preparing and following up after the event
- One event can cost around $10,000

More experiential, personal, and interactive.

Many event organizers simply pack up and go home, missing key opportunities to connect with attendees after the event.

Continued communication with attendees is crucial in creating loyal attendees, customers

Have multiple goals rather than one....assure success

Prep – send out invitations mail or email set up appointment...focus your special

Perception is everything

Never sit down

Table should never be a wall separating you for the attendees

Avoid. Pitch posture

- Practice being comfortable
- No radar vision – focus on who you are talking with.
- No cell calls
- No eating or drinking that is visible to the attendees

Opening lines:

- What brings you to the show today?

Notes

_____

_____

_____

_____

_____

_____

_____

_____

_____

_____

_____

_____

_____

_____

_____

_____

Chapter 5:
Trade Show Budgets and Proposals/
Start Planning.

Trade Show Yearly Budget

Itemized	Projected	Actual
Travel	_____	_____
Lodging	_____	_____
Meals	_____	_____
Entertainment	_____	_____
(Clients & Prospects)		
Staff Salaries	_____	_____
Promotional items	_____	_____
Print Promotional materials	_____	_____
Shipping	_____	_____
Electric (floor work In & Out)	_____	_____
Installment & Dismantle	_____	_____
Furniture rental	_____	_____
Flower rental	_____	_____
Patting rental	_____	_____
Lead retrieval fee	_____	_____
Internet service fee	_____	_____
Cable TV rental fee	_____	_____
Carpet rental	_____	_____
Drayage	_____	_____
(material handling – In & Out)		
Total	_____	_____

Trade Show Proposal

Event: _____ Date: _____

Sponsor: _____

_____

Location: _____

Target Audience: _____

_____

Projected Investment: _____

Staff Involved: # _____

- Sales: _____
- Ambassador(s) _____

Benefit: _____

_____

_____

Pre-event Strategy: _____

_____

Objectives: _____

_____

Follow-up Plan: _____

_____

Target Number of New Prospects:_____

Specific Prospects: _____

_____

_____

_____

Trade Show
Individual Show Budget

Event: _____   Date: _____

Sponsor: _____

_____

Location: _____

Staff Involved: # _____

- Sales: _____
- Ambassador(s) _____

Itemized

	Projected	Actual
Travel	_____	_____
Lodging	_____	_____
Meals	_____	_____
Entertainment	_____	_____
(Clients & Prospects)		
Staff Salaries	_____	_____
Promotional items	_____	_____
Print Promotional materials	_____	_____
Shipping	_____	_____
Electric (floor work In & Out)	_____	_____
Installment & Dismantle	_____	_____
Furniture rental	_____	_____
Flower rental	_____	_____
Patting rental	_____	_____

Lead retrieval fee   _____   _____

Internet service fee   _____   _____

Cable TV rental fee   _____   _____

Carpet rental   _____   _____

Drayage   _____   _____
(Material Handling – In & Out)

Total   _____   _____

Start Planning

Check List and Plan

Purpose: _____

_____

_____

Booth Size: _____

Signage: _____

Target Clients & Prospects: _____

_____

_____

_____

Promotional Materials: _____

_____

_____

_____

Freebies/Products: _____

_____

_____

Special gifts & targeted individuals: _____

_____

_____

Prep Work: _____

_____

_____

_____

_____

Follow-up Plan: _____

_____

_____

_____

Staffing:

Sales staff: _____

_____

Ambassador: _____

_____

Chapter 6:
Exhibit Booths and Opportunities

Often Trade Shows offer seminars, demonstrations of products, and raffles geared to the demographics of the target participants.

Exhibitor Booth

Most common standard exhibit booths include

- 10' x 10' space
- (1) small company sign with booth number
- (2) side 3' high pipe & drapes and (1) 10' back pipe & drape
- (1) 6 or 8-foot shirted table
- (1-2) chairs
- (1) small trash can

Be Inquisitive – ASK

Although there is no guarantee, it does not hurt to ask.

- Ask for specifics (cost, booth size, and what is included in the price) trade shows are not all the same.
- Ask what the number of exhibitors have been at previous trade shows and number projected.
- Ask for the list of previous exhibitors.
- Ask for the number of attendees who attended the previous year.
- Ask can exhibitors negotiate for a larger space.
- Ask if there are opportunities for speaking or product demonstraions.
- Ask if there is an opportunity to select your booth location.

Sponsorship Opportunities

- Often include advertising opportunities, higher visibility, opportunity to select your booth location and speaking opportunities.
- There are often 2 – 4 sponsorship levels which typically include advertising opportunities, higher visibility, opportunity to select both booth location and speaking opportunities.
- Often trade shows offer various events and activities and look for participating companies to sponsor these events which in turn offer yet another opportunity to draw attention to your company.

Stand Out

- Embrace the trade show theme, season, or holiday, when possible, to heighten the appeal of your booth.
- Consider
  - Interactive games or demonstrations
  - Videos of services, testimonials, product demonstration
  - Promotional materials – be cautious and not overly anxious to distribute unrequested information. Keep in mind 85% of printed materials are trashed.

Connections

- Tip – staple key prospects' business cards to 3x5 cards and note personal information, shared needs, and level of interest to reference in follow-up correspondence. Personalizing correspondence will remind the prospect of your prior interaction opening the door for further correspondence and a stronger likelihood of a sale or working together.

Chapter 7:
Create Trade Show Booths
with a WOW Factor

As trade show booth camp coach and a professional speaker, I have spent a great deal of time working with clients and observing trade show booths and staff. You may find these tips rather simply, yet a surprising number of companies, associations and business owners are failing to see that these tips are the key to developing the foundation of a successful trade show booth.

Create a booth environment which taps
all of the senses of the attendees.

1. Keep your company logo and tag line centered at the top of your display.

2. Post 2- 4 key bullet points (addressing needs and outcomes) in the middle panel of the display.

3. Keep your space clean and tidy. Avoid having garbage lying around (cups, candy wrappers, items left by attendees etc.).

4. Text – keep it simple, bold, concise, and in large font. You want prospects able to read it from outside the booth.

5. Keep it open – avoid placing the table in front of the booth creating a barrier. Consider placing the table either to the back of the space or on either side of the booth. This creates a warm, open, inviting space.

6. Graphics/Photos – be selective choose bold, colorful, engaging items that compliment your brand and key bullet points.

7. Color scheme – select colors that either represent your company's logo or compliments the company's logo, brand, and image. Be cautious not to invest in trendy colors as they change frequently. Displays are a rather costly invest, not something you want to replace often.

8. Theme – occasionally trade shows adopt a theme and ask exhibitors to incorporate the theme in their displays. When planning do not lose sight of your company's brand or image. Considers well placed decorative items, a specialty centerpiece, or a raffle gift in line with the theme. Remember "less is best".

9. Do it right or not at all – be prepared to invest the funds to create a quality professional display that represents the image the company wants to project.

10. Lead Management – consider renting or purchasing electronic lead machines, enter data right into your computer on site or gather business cards.

11. Be provocative – write content that entices, challenges and addresses what is in it for the attendees company, association, or business.

12. Audio/Visuals – these can be attraction grabbing to entice the attendees creating a desire and an opportunity to highlight your company's products or services. You could also show demonstrations and testimonials.

13. Add lighting – to light feature key point or graphics which you want to capture the attention of the attendees.

14. Make the booth interactive and playful - be cautious not to lose sight of your purpose and goals at the event.

If you incorporate these practical tips in your planning you will create a strong interesting engaging memorable booth. Your clients and prospects will be attracted to your booth and never want to leave.

Chapter 8:
Freebies Promotional Items vs. Actual Products

Your company may want to consider offering actual product samples rather than the typical freebie promotional items at the next tradeshow if:

- Your products are not already on store shelves.

  - Free products (sample size) may pique interest and desire.
  - This may encourage prospective clients /customers to begin requesting the product prompting retailers to start carry the product.

- Your products are not presently available – free samples may increase the public awareness.
- Understand: Every tradeshow participant will not necessarily be interested or desire your product(s) or services even if it is offered free.

  - Be selective and not waste time and the free product on window shoppers or "trick or treaters" who are not interested.
  - With your ideal prospect take the time to create a connection and offer the product as a token of your appreciation for their time and interest.

- Developing partnerships with other companies/businesses that offer product(s) and services that compliment your products and services and have similar ideal clients/ customer.

  - Consider each company agreeing to offer each others company's free sample products or services (discounted)

- It is equally important to accompany the free samples with product literature.

Freebies have their place and benefit if:

- You are a new business and want to cast a wide net announcing the opening.
    - Consider a free promotion item with your company logo, website, and contact information.
    - Consider pens, magnets, eyes glass clean, chap sticks,
- You are launching a new product or services and want many attendees to stop by your booth even if not necessarily.

Chapter 9:
Sending the Best – Selecting the Ideal Trade Show Team

Consider these six key questions when selecting individuals for your Trade Show Team

1. Does the trade show require Ambassadors (Mission: Establish relationships & strengthen your brand or Sales Force (Mission: Sell, sell, and sell) or both?

2. How suitable and prepared are the individuals to represent your business or corporation?

3. How knowledgeable are the individuals about your products/services?

4. How effective are the individuals at identifying ideal prospects?

5. How effective are the individuals in attracting prospects?

6. Are the individuals introverts or extroverts?

Notes

_____

_____

_____

_____

_____

_____

_____

_____

_____

_____

_____

_____

_____

_____

_____

_____

_____

Chapter 10:
Common Characteristics
of Successful Trade Show Teams

Here are five common characteristics of successful trade show teams.

Top Teams take risks.

They search and embrace new things, are experimental, change things up and set their eyes on big clients. I once met a millionaire businessman and asked him how he built his million dollar business. He said "I sought out opportunities to fail at." He immediately noticed the puzzled look on my face and elaborated "If I only sought opportunities that I would succeed at I would have tried very few things. The more opportunities I pursued and risks I took the more I learned. In turn the more I learned the more successful I became."

Top Teams use their time wisely.

Top performing teams are made up of individuals who are well organized and particular about how they use their time both prior to and during trade shows, to get the best return on their investment. Ideally, they spend the majority of their floor time with clients that have the highest payoff. Average performing teams spend too much time with marginal opportunities (window shoppers, trick-or-treaters) that consume time with little if any return.

Top Teams invest in themselves, their clients and prospects.

Top performing individuals and teams recognize the benefit of investing their time and money to make trade shows memorable. They purchase gifts that are about their clients or prospects, not the company they represent. They take the necessary time to learn about their clients' needs and concerns. They are committed to learning new ideas and techniques to enhance their expertise by purchasing and exchanging among themselves relevant books, podcast programs and best practices. They attend seminars and workshops, purchase industry magazines and use the Internet to keep abreast of the trends in their niche market.

Top Performers and Teams are passionate about Networking and Selling.

A typical trade show team consists of one or more individuals. The highly motivated teams are passionate, actively attract and engage individuals to discuss their products and services. These individuals thrive on meeting new people, making contacts and selling. Less effective individuals shy away from interacting, appear to be shy or would rather be somewhere else. They don't like initiating conversations and don't like meeting new prospects.

Top Performing Teams seek the audience of Top Performers.

There is no better place to be than with others who possess the same characteristics, goals and commitment to learn, grow and succeed. That is why it is beneficial to know who your ideal clients are and be selective about which of your clients, prospects, and partners you choose.

Chapter 11:
Working the Crowd – Eight Interactive Tips to Interact and Engage with Prospects

Be Prepared and Present

- Wear comfort clothing.
- Arrange and take time to eat meals.
- Arrive early to be properly set-up.
- When possible, set-up your booth the day before the event.
- Avoid late night partying.
- Be actively engaged and focused.

    Key: Be well rested, energized, and prepared

Be inviting and approachable

Projecting an inviting affect (facial expressions, body language and eye contact) is key to attracting attendees to visit your booth. It is extremely important to appear both open to engage in conversation and willing to share information and answer questions.

- Dress for the audience and the event.
- Make eye contact and smile as people are approaching your booth.
- Be "Real" expose your "Personhood."
- Be consistent – treat everyone in the same manner.
- Not all people that pass by your booth have a need or interest in your product or service. Smile, nod or say hello indicating you see them. Conserve your energy.

    Key: Be consistent treat everyone the same

Listen and then listen more

Welcome the guest and be patient, allow the prospect to direct the conversation. Start with silence and implement the 80/20 rule. Spend 80% of the time together encouraging and letting them identify their concerns, wants, and needs and learning about their company (services & products). This will help establish a workable relationship and focus on their needs, concerns, and challenges. Use 20% sharing the information about your company's services/products. Be relevant, soft-sell, and build a relationship.

- Create a warm, relaxing, comfortable trusting relationship.
- Identify their core concerns, needs, and wants.
- Focus intently on them and avoid looking over their shoulder scanning the crowd for the next prospect.

> Key: Rephrase what has been shared—to assure the potential client you are engaged.

Get Off the Topic

Alternate the conversation between business and general conversation topics. Not too personal but general simple questions. Be open and inquisitive.

This can be as simply as:

- What brought you to this event?
- What do you think of the trade show/expo?
- What break-out sessions have you attended?
- What did you think of the keynote speaker?

> Key: Listen, focus, and ask pertinent questions

Offer affirmation and compliments

Everyone needs and enjoys having their ego stroked. This can be accomplished by being observant.

- Point out and compliment their jewelry, watch, haircut, style, briefcase, or other personal attributes.
- Ask for their opinion re: the industry, trends.
- Acknowledge and thank them for sharing their expertise and experience.

> Key: Be sincere

Ask open ended questions

Once a prospect shares their needs, concerns, or wants it is your responsibility to demonstrate you have clearly listened and care about what they are sharing.

Avoid questions which can be answered with "yes" or "no." Craft your questions to identify their fear, concerns and needs. What product or service is your company presently using? How is your company presently managing X now?

- Do not assume you know more than those attending the event.
- Some people are humble and do not expose the depth of their knowledge.

> Key: Getting them to freely share their concerns, needs and wants. You can provide the first aide to address them.

Wrap-up

Enthusiastically thank the guest for choosing to visit your booth and inquire about your services/products. If you feel during your interaction the guest is a strong prospect request their business cards. Jot down a few key personal items and business needs and concerns shared on the card or a separate piece of paper.

Closing comments.

- "It was an honor and pleasure meeting you."
- "Enjoy visiting the other booths."
- "Feel free to stop by again if you have additional questions."

> Key: Be appreciative and thankful.

Follow-up

Have a detailed follow-up plan of action established prior to the event.

Send a personalized follow-up thank you card, or letter handwritten or typed rather than email to stand out from other companies.

- Be sure to include a few of the personal comments you learned about them to strengthen the connection.
- Include information about how your company's services/products.
- It would be an honor and pleasure working with you.
- I welcome scheduling call to explore how we might work together.
- I will contact you within 2 weeks to formally schedule a call.

> Key: Be proactive and implement your plan in a timely manner.

Ultimate Goal: Initiate, establish and reinforce the connection.

Taking the time to think, plan and create an enticing interactive trade show booth and train your employees to attract and engage prospective leads are the keys to effectively working a trade show. If you incorporate these tips in your planning, you will create a strong, memorable booth and are more likely to attract interested prospects.

Chapter 12:
Make Your Personal Connection
So Engaging Clients Never Want To Leave.

"I feel like you really understand our needs!"

"This has really been both a pleasure and beneficial!"

"I am so glad I took the time to stop by your booth!"

Have you heard these comments from you clients as much as you desire?

The challenge with attracting prospective clients at trade shows is making the connection *more*. More appealing. More playful. More engaging. More about them than the company you represent. More memorable.

Remember: It is about them and creating a memorable connection.

The key is to realize that people are quick to judge and you have about 10 seconds to attract their attention and make them feel welcomed.

Here are three practices to make your connection so engaging that clients don't want to leave your booth, will revisit your booth and bring colleagues by to visit.

Reminisce. Revisit Your Past.

Do an internal audit of the previous year's best and worst trade show experiences. Which three or four were the most beneficial shows. *The shows that left you exhilarated because you interacted with many visitors? The ones you were surprised the time pasted so quickly.* What made these shows so exciting and engaging? Was it the booth design? Was it freebies you distributed? Was it the staff you sent?

Take the time to:

- List the three or four shows that couldn't end quickly enough? What made these shows so irritating, miserable, and uneventful? Was it the location? Was the wrong team sent? Was it a lack of trade show experience or training? Was it a poor selection of a trade show?
- Make a list of the behaviors, situations, attitude of the best and worst trade show experience. Are there noted patterns or commonalities? Now take a step back and ask yourself how well I routinely prepare, evaluate, and select staff and set goals for trade shows. If your answer is "not well" here is what you can do.

It should be all about them; not you and your company.
Believe me business owners, CEOs and consumers in general really could care less about you or your company. *They care about them. They are consumed about their needs and concerns.* They care about getting what they need for the best price, quality and customer service. So perhaps the best use of your prep time should be to make a list of all the things prospects could care less about.

Think of it this way:

- Consumers do not care about you.
- Some people are simply "*window shopping*" no desire or plan to buy anything.
- Some people are simply there to "trick or treat", desiring "*only*" the freebies.

Try these probing questions and comments when interacting with clients and prospects:

- What are the biggest challenges your company/business is facing today?
- What has been tried before?
- How would the company/business condition improve if these were improved?

- How important are these needs: (on a scale of 1 – 10)
- The three questions you need to ask yourself are…
- Here's the good news…

They want content. They want relevant, practical, concise information and solutions to their needs and concerns. *That is what prospects want. That is what companies, associations and business owners want.* When they are reading your display text, viewing your video demonstrations and listening to your pitch, they need to be thinking to themselves, "We need this, this solves our problems, tell me more."

- Do your homework and be selective
  - ◆ Take the necessary time to research each event
    - Is it my niche market
    - Will key decision makers be attending
- Ask yourself
  - ◆ Will participating generate a return on my invest
  - ◆ What are our measurable goals
    - Sales
    - Positioning
    - Assess this new market/event
- Select and Assign the team
  - ◆ Sales Force Only – *Mission: Sell, sell, sell* – Decision makers & management level attending Only
  - ◆ Ambassador(s) Only – *Mission: establish relationships, strengthen your brand, promote your product and services* – No decision makers attending event
  - ◆ Sales Force & Ambassador Team – Decision makers/ management and support employees attending. Send Sales Force back on the road once Decision Makers session is finished and Ambassadors staff the booth for remainder of event.

Notes

Chapter 13:
Trade Show Survival Kit

As the Boy Scout Slogan states "Be Prepared," you just never know what you may need.

Here are items exhibitors may want to have on hand to address any minor injuries, accidents, and mishaps.

Create your personal Trade Show Survival Kit.

Change of Shoes	Dental Floss
Change of Clothing	Sewing Kit
Super Glue	Eye Drops
Glue Stick	Stapler & Staples
Sanitizer Wipes	Hand Sanitizer
Cough Drops	Breath Mints
First Aid Kit	Small Pocket Knife
Scissors	Travel Raincoat
Small Mirror	Travel Umbrella
Chap Stick	Hand Lotion
Tide Stick	Tylenol
Mask(s)	Windex / 409 Cleaner
Nail File	Measuring Tape
Nail Clipper	Eye Glass Repair Kit
Tissues	Eye Glass Cleaning cloth
Safety Pins	Eye Glass Cleaner
Regular Tape	Masking Tape
Universal Electric Plug	Power Strip
Power Bank Charger	Small extension cord

Notes

Chapter 14:
Virtual Trade Show Tips

The virtual trade show is not any different than the one you might set up in a conference hall. Well, besides the fact that it is not an in-person event and that you are not setting up banners, tables, and collateral. The reality is that the virtual trade show involves just as much strategic planning and set up. You may not be schlepping boxes of brochures and candy into a building, but you will be spending just as much time and effort in preparation for the virtual event.

The goal of any trade show is to meet with interested attendees and to capture leads for follow up conversations. Take all the strategies you use for in-person events and creatively shift them to the virtual world.

Here are some key strategies to keep in mind as you prepare for your virtual trade show:

1) The Virtual Booth

Online trade shows come in all shapes and sizes. Meeting planners and organizations have a variety of different platforms to host the show. Some of the platforms are simple, some are overly complex. Your goal is to use whichever platform you are given and make the experience as simple as you can for the attendees that stop by your booth.

You have three options to consider when it comes to setting up your booth:

A) Good — An unstaffed static branded page that offers basic info, a website link, and show promotional offer.

B) Better — An unstaffed page that has a branded video, prize drawing, link to more information, and a direct link to a staffed virtual meeting room where they can visit with someone at that moment.

C) BEST — Be there "virtually in-person" to greet, meet, and engage. Be prepared to share a screen, video, or to lead them to a virtual meeting room.

2) The Virtual Meeting Room

Your goal is not to hand out virtual candy! Your goal is to have meaningful conversations with attendees. The best way to accomplish that is to bring them up close. What strategies or intrigue do you display at an in-person booth to get people to stop by? Come up with a virtual equivalent. Then encourage them to join you in a virtual meeting room for that conversation.

Use the following ideas:

- A link to join a virtual meeting room (your preferred video conferencing tool).
- Staff that room to meet people.
- (Break Time) — When you will not be in the room to visit in-person, make sure you offer 1) A list on your virtual booth page of the times you will be available, 2) provide a pre-scheduled option for them to choose an appointment.

Do not have the virtual meeting room available if you are not going to staff it. Attendees grow quickly agitated when they take the digital steps to get to you and no one is present. You will lose the lead if you make things complicated.

3) Think Like A Producer: "Lights, Camera, Audio!"

A successful in-person trade show booth has visual appeal with color, lighting, and a branded message that appeals to the need of the attendee. The virtual trade show booth requires the same thoughtful set up.

You are not simply managing a trade show booth, you have become a virtual presenter!

Think about your booth in terms of a presentation — just as if you were the keynote speaker or a breakout session presenter. You can consider your trade show investment a total loss if all you provide is a PowerPoint show, bullet points, and a talking head! You must view the virtual booth and experience from the perspective of the "audience member." The attendees are used to being entertained by that screen they are watching. And they have grown accustomed to a level of quality production. Your virtual booth will miss the mark if you do not meet the following expectations:

- Lights — Invest in good lighting for your video conferencing. Minimize the shadows on your face.
- Audio — Attendees will forgive so-so lighting, but they will not tolerate bad audio. Set up a dependable microphone and test the volume.
- Camera — You might be able to use the default camera on your computer or mobile device. However, for a quality broadcast image you will want to invest in a dedicated camera. (Production Note: position the camera so that you are looking directly into the lens.)
- Reliable Internet Connection — Do not compromise. Use a direct ethernet connection and do not depend on Wi-Fi.

4) Your Task is to Ask

Remember that your goal is to have meaningful conversations that lead to future opportunities. You will not achieve that goal if you turn your virtual room into a show & tell pitch. The attendee will take a virtual walk the moment you shift into a selling position. Use the time you have with those who stop by to find out about them and their needs. Ask and listen. You can then tailor your responses (and your follow up) to the specific concerns they have and how you can help.

5) Collateral & Swag

Yes — you should be prepared to hand out "virtual candy, pens & journals, and stress balls." It will not actually be those things, but you can engage your visitor by having ready a digital one-sheet with more information which they can download on the spot.

And when it comes to swag, go ahead and plan on giving gifts to the attendees who stop by your booth. Attendees that express interest in your service/product will be surprised when you go the extra mile and send to them a genuine tangible gift. Follow-up by mailing them a treat or traditional swag. Send a handwritten thank you note for their interest and time.

6) Video Follow Up

You want your virtual trade show booth to stand out in the crowded virtual hall. But, more importantly, you want to create a strong impression that builds a personal and professional connection after the show. Send an email with a personalized 1–2-minute video for each lead. Mention them by name and thank them for "stopping by.

The extra mile is not crowded with your competitors, so make the effort and lead the way!

Steven Iwerson, CSP™
CEO & President
Aurora Pointe, LLC

Chapter 15:
Traveling Trade Show Booth

It is not uncommon to find me at the local Panera or Barnes and Noble café, either in my hometown or in the town I am working in. Not only do I get my caffeine fix for the day, along with access to free Wi-Fi, I also get the opportunity to attract prospects for the various facets of my business. Coffee shops have proven to be ideal locations to promote myself and my services.

Trade shows can provide corporations, small businesses and associations with a wonderful opportunity to spread the word to their target audience(s), enhance relationships with current clients and offer the time to establish relationships with receptive new prospects. The key is getting more quality, relaxed face time with ideal prospects. Trade shows are not cheap by any means, considering travel expenses, hotel accommodations, booth cost, and meals.

I have taken the traditional trade show format to virtually everywhere I travel and work from the local coffee shop to restaurants and airports throughout the country.

Creating a Traveling Trade Show Booth

Suggested supplies and materials needed:

1. A few current copies of your professional association's magazine, your business newsletter or other periodicals related to your expertise/industries.

2. A name tag on your briefcase (on one side your business card & the other side business/association logo) place brief case in a prominent position near you, revealing either side of the tag.

3. Trade Show Briefcase – be sure to situate the bag so that the logo is visible.

   - Purchase a briefcase with your company's logo or name on the outside of the bag.
   - Consider using your association's national or state convention bag.

4. A few small promotional items (newsletters, brochures etc.).

5. A few business cards.

Display all the above fairly organized but not so that it looks staged. The objective is to subtly prompt curiosity from bystanders who may scan your mini trade show booth while passing by. While working, occasional glance at the promotional items, to suggest you need to refer to the items, which often draws more attention to you, heightens curiosity and prompts questions.

Areas ideal for Mini traveling trade shows

- Airport gates – use the seat next to you or the floor
- Airport restaurants/bars – while dining or coping with long layovers
- Planes – using seat trays
- Coffee shops & bookstore cafes
- Waiting rooms – use the seat next to you or the floor

After one year of implementing a "traveling trade show" I was able to directly link two speaking engagements, five coaching clients, one long term consulting client and bartered an office & clerical services.

There are no boundaries to where you can promote your products and services so be creative, bold and adventurous.

Glossary

A

A/V: Audio/visual support such as television monitors, VCRs, or taped music.

A/V Contractor: A supplier of audio/visual equipment and services.

Advance Order: An order for services sent to the service contractor prior to the installation date. Compare with Floor Order.

Advance Rates: Fees associated with advance orders, which typically include discounts when paid in advance.

Advance Receiving: Location set by show management to receive freight before the start of show. Freight is stored at this location and then shipped to the show at the appropriate time.

Aisle: A walkway intended for audience movement through an exposition or exhibit.

B

Back wall: The panels at the rear of an exhibit.

Back wall Exhibit: An exhibit that is back-to-back with another exhibit or against a building wall.

Banner: A suspended panel used as a decoration or a sign, usually made of fabric or paper for temporary use.

Bill of Lading (B/L): A document that establishes the terms between a shipper and a transportation company for the transport of goods between specified points for a specified charge. Also see Air Waybill, Inland Bill of Lading, Ocean Bill of Lading, and Through Bill of Lading.

Blueprint: A scale drawing of booth space layout, construction, and specifications.

Boneyard: A storage area for empty crates and contractor materials.

Booth: An area made up of one or more standard units of exhibit space.

Booth Area: The amount of floor space assigned to an exhibitor.

Booth Number: A number assigned by show management to identify an exhibitor's floor space.

Booth Personnel: Staff members assigned by an exhibitor to work in an exhibit.

Booth Size: The dimensions of the floor space contracted by an exhibitor. Usually sold in 10' x 10' increments.

C

C.I.F. (Cost, Insurance, Freight): A pricing term indicating that these charges are included in the stated price.

Carpenter: A skilled worker used to uncrate, install, dismantle, and recrate exhibit properties.

Carpet Tape: Double-sided tape used to adhere the edge of a carpet to the floor.

Carrier: A transportation line moving freight. Usually a van line, common carrier, rail line, or air carrier. Also see Common Carrier.

Collective Agreement: A contract between an employer and a union specifying the terms and conditions for employment, the status of the union, and the process for settling disputes during the contract period. Also known as Labor Agreement, Union Contract.

Column: A pillar in an exposition facility which supports the roof or other overhead structures. Usually shown on a floor plan as a solid square.

Common Carrier: A transportation company moving people or goods. For exhibit freight, the carrier usually accepts only crated materials and consolidates the properties of several customers into one shipment bound for the same destination.

Construction Drawing: A drawing which gives detailed diagrams and instructions for building an exhibit.

Contractor: An individual or company that provides services or materials to a trade show and/or its exhibitors. Also see Official Contractor, Exhibitor Appointed Contractor.

Corner Booth: An exhibit space with exposure on at least two aisles.

Custom Exhibit: A display designed and built to meet the specific needs of an exhibitor.

CWT: Hundred weight. A measurement used for shipping exhibit properties. Usually 100 pounds.

D

D.T. Labor: Double Time Labor. Work performed on overtime and charged at twice the published rate.

Damage Report: A report submitted by an exhibitor to a freight company or drayage contractor itemizing damage to shipped goods.

Dead Time: Time when a worker is unable to perform duties due to factors beyond his or her control.

Declared Value: A shipper's stated dollar value for the contents of a shipment.

Decorator: An individual (skilled craftsperson) or company (a contractor) providing services for a trade show and/or its exhibitors.

DIM Weight: Length x width x height divided by 194 for domestic shipments, or divided by 166 for international shipments.

Dismantle: To take apart an exhibit. Also known as Take-down, Teardown.

Display Rules & Regulations: Exhibit construction specifications endorsed by major exhibit industry associations. Also the specific set of rules that apply to an exposition.

Dock: A platform where freight is loaded onto and removed from vehicles or vessels.

Drayage: The movement of show materials from shipping dock to booth for show set up and back to dock for return shipment at end of show.

Drayage Contractor: A company responsible for handling exhibit materials at a trade show.

Drayage Form: A form completed by an exhibitor requesting handling of materials.

E

Easel: A stand for displaying objects.

Electrical Contractor: A company hired by show management to provide electrical services to exhibitors.

End Cap: An exhibit space with aisles on three sides.

Est. Wt.: Estimated Weight.

Event Marketing: Face-to-face promotional experiences between customers and companies.

Exhibit Directory: A guide for exhibition attendees which lists exhibitors and exhibit locations.

Exhibit Hall: The area(s) within an exposition center where exhibits are located.

Exhibit Manager: Person in charge of a company's exhibit program.

Exhibitor Appointed Contractor: A contractor hired by an exhibitor to perform trade show services independently of show management appointed contractors. Also called Independent Contractor, EAC.

Exhibitor Kit: A package of information which contains all rules, regulations, and forms relating to an exhibition, provided to exhibitors by show management. Also called Service Kit.

Exposition Rules: The set of regulations which govern a given trade show.

F

Fabrication: The construction of an exhibit.

Fire Lane: An aisle that must be kept clear of obstructions to allow emergency egress.

Fire Retardant: Term used to describe a finish which coats materials with a fire-resistant (not fire proof) cover.

Floor Manager: An individual representing show management who is responsible for the exhibition area.

Floor Marking: Method used to mark booth spaces.

Floor Order: Order for services placed after exhibit installation has begun. Compare with Advance Order.

Floor Plan: A map showing the size and locations of exhibit spaces.

Forklift, Fork truck: Motorized vehicle used to load, unload, and transport heavy items.

Foul Bill of Lading: A carrier-issued receipt indicating that transported merchandise was damaged when received. Compare with Clean Bill of Lading.

Four Hour Call: Minimum work period for which union labor must be paid.

Freight: Exhibit properties and other materials shipped for an exhibit.

Freight Desk: The area where inbound and outbound exhibit materials are handled at a trade show.

G

General Contractor: Show management appointed company providing services to a trade show and/or its exhibitors. Also called Official Contractor. Compare with Exhibitor Appointed Contractor.

Graphic: A photo, copy panel, or artwork applied to an exhibit.

H

Hall: General term used for an exposition facility or the exhibit area within a facility.

Hand Truck: Small hand-propelled vehicle used for transporting small loads.

Hard wall: A type of exhibit construction in which walls are made of a solid material, rather than fabric.

Header: A sign or other structure across the top of an exhibit.

I

I&D: Installation & Dismantle (of an exhibit). Also known as Set Up and Take-down.

Independent Contractor: A contractor hired by an exhibitor to perform trade show services independently of show management appointed contractors.

*Also called Exhibitor Appointed Contractor, EAC.

Infringement: An exhibitor's unauthorized use of floor space outside the leased booth area..

In-line: An exhibit that is constructed in a continuous line along an aisle.

*Also called Linear Display.

Installation: The process of setting up exhibit properties according to specifications.

*Also called Assembly, Set Up.

Installation & Dismantle: The set up and take-down of exhibits. Also called I & D.

Island Exhibit; A display with aisles on four sides.

K

K.D. (Knockdown): An exhibit with separate components that must be assembled on-site.

L

Labor: Contracted workers who perform services. Also called Craftspersons.

Labor Call: (1) Method of securing union employees. (2) Time specified for labor to report (as in a 7 A.M. call). (3) Minimum amount for which labor must be paid.

Labor Desk: Exhibit hall location where exhibitors may place orders for labor.

Labor Form: The form used by exhibitors to order labor.

Lead Tracking: A manual or automated system used to conduct follow-up activities for sales prospects resulting from a trade show.

Less than Truckload (LTL): The rate charged for freight weighing less than the minimum weight for a truckload.

Light Box: An enclosure which contains lighting underneath a translucent facing material. Used to back-light signs or graphics applied to the face.

Lighting: The amount or type of illumination in an exhibit or exhibition hall.

Linear Display: An exhibit that is constructed in a continuous line along an aisle. Also called In-line.

Loading Dock: An area within an exposition facility where freight is received and shipped.

Lock-Up: A secure storage area within an exposition facility.

Logo: A specific symbol chosen to represent a company. Usually comprised of stylized type alone or in conjunction with graphic art.

M

Marshaling Yard: A lot where trucks gather for orderly dispatch to show site.

Modular Exhibit: An exhibit constructed with interchangeable components designed to be set up in various arrangements and sizes.

Move-in: The date specified by show management for beginning exhibit installation.

Move-out: The date specified by show management for dismantling exhibits.

Multimedia: Combining two or more types of audio/visual support in a presentation.

N

Net Square Footage: The total amount of leased booth space in an exposition facility.

O

O.T. Labor: Work performed on overtime.

Official Contractor: Show management appointed company providing services to a trade show and/or its exhibitors. Also called General Contractor. Compare with Exhibitor Appointed Contractor.

On-site Order; Floor order placed at a show site.

Overtime: A designation for work performed outside the hours specified as normal working hours. Usually work performed on overtime is charged at a substantially higher rate.

P

P.W.: Packed Weight.

Packing List: A document prepared by a shipper itemizing contents of shipment and including other information needed by the carrier.

Peninsula Display: An exhibit with aisles on three sides.

Perimeter Booth: A booth space on a outside wall.

Pipe & Drape: Tubing covered with draped fabric to make up the rails and back wall of a trade show.

Podium: A demonstration area, usually higher than the surrounding floor.

Portable Exhibit: A lightweight display unit that can be moved without a forklift.

Power Strip: A movable unit having multiple electrical outlets.

Prefab: A pre-built exhibit ready for installation.

Press Kit: A package of materials put together for the media. Usually a folder containing press releases, product announcements, and other materials.

Press Release: An article submitted to the media for publication. Usually announcing news about a product, company, or individual.

Q

Quad Box: Four electrical outlets in one box.

R

Rail: A low wall used to divide exhibits.

Rental Booth: A complete booth package offered to exhibitors on a rental basis.

Return Panels: Side panels joined perpendicular to the backwall.

Rigger: A skilled worker responsible for handling and assembly of machinery.

Right To Work State: A state where no person can be denied the right to work because of membership or non-membership in a labor union.

S

S.T. Labor: Straight Time Labor. Work performed during normal work hours at the standard rate. Compare with D.T. Labor, Overtime.

Security Cages: Cages provided to exhibitors for locking up materials.

Service Desk: The location at which exhibitors order services from show management.

Service Kit: A packet of show-related information and order forms provided to exhibitors by show management. Also called Exhibitor Kit.

Set Up: The process of erecting an exhibit from its components. Also called Assembly, Installation.

Set-up Drawing: Drawings which give detailed instructions for the installation of an exhibit.

Show Break: Time specified for the closing of an exhibition and beginning of dismantling.

Show Decorator: A company or individual responsible for providing draping, carpeting, and signage services for the trade show and its exhibitors.

Show Manager: The organizer and operator of an exposition..

Show Rules: The general rules and regulations governing a specific trade show.

Shrink Wrap: A process used to seal materials in transparent plastic.

Skirting: Decorative covering around tables and risers.

Sparky: Electrician

Special Handling: Applies to exhibit shipments requiring extra labor, equipment, or time for delivery to exhibit space.

Swag: Stuff We All Get, or Stuff We All Giveaway.

T

Table Top Display
An exhibit designed for use on the top of a table or similar surface.

Talent: An individual or company hired to work in an exhibit to greet visitors, demonstrate product, or stage a performance.

Target Date: A date set by show management for the arrival of freight at a trade show. Usually shipments received before or after this date are assessed a penalty charge.

Teardown: The dismantling of an exhibit. Also known as Take-down.

Terminal: Freight handling or dock area.

Trade Show: An exposition related to a particular industry or group, and open only to the members of that group.

Traffic Flow: The movement of visitors through an exposition or exhibit.

U

Union: An organization of workers formed with the purpose of protecting workers' rights and increasing bargaining power with an employer on such issues as wages, hours, and benefits.

Union Steward: An on-site union official elected by coworkers to oversee a particular union's work in a facility and resolve any disputes over union jurisdiction. Also known as Shop Steward.

V

Velcro: The trade name for a fabric closure with two components: hooks and loops. The two components adhere when pressed together and separate when pulled apart, allowing repeated use.

Visqueen: A clear plastic sheeting that is placed over exhibit carpeting after its laid in order to protect it until the show opens. Visqueen also allows exhibit components to slide on top of it during setup, allowing you to align various exhibit components by simply pushing them into position.

W

Work Rules: Regulations that specify the conditions of a craftsperson's labor, including work hours and pay structure.

Work Time: The period of paid time which begins when craftspersons are turned over to an exhibitor and ends when they are released by the exhibitor.

Biography

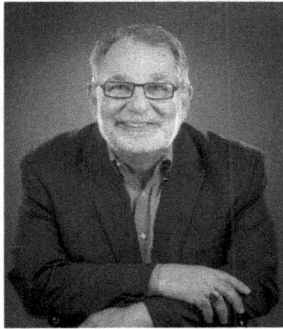

Richard Avdoian is founder and CEO of Midwest Business Institute, a leadership coaching, consulting, and training group, in Metro St. Louis.

He works with businesses, corporations and associations committed to training, and retaining highly motivated productive employees. He is an employee development expert who specializes in enhancing employee potential and maximizing capabilities to provide exemplary customer service and increase productivity and profitability.

He has worked extensively in the behavioral health field and with clients in over forty different industries providing programs and services in teamwork, leadership, employee development and customer service.

Avdoian's credentials for employee development and teamwork expertise rank him among the top speakers in the United States and form the foundation for his ability to deliver excellent material.

To purchase copies of Successfully Working Trade Shows or other books and products, contact Richard at Richard@RichardAvdoian.com.

Interested in having Richard speak or present training to your company, corporation or association? Learn more about his programs and services at www.RichardAvdoian.com.

www.ingramcontent.com/pod-product-compliance
Lightning Source LLC
Chambersburg PA
CBHW061050220326
41597CB00018BA/2743